Fearless Prospecting: How to Win Clients When You Need It Most

Copyright © 2024 Reginaldo Osnildo
All rights reserved.

PRESENTATION

INTRODUCTION TO ACTIVE PROSPECTION

CHANGING YOUR MINDSET ABOUT SALES

IDENTIFICATION OF THE TARGET AUDIENCE

BUILDING YOUR SALES CONFIDENCE

DEVELOPING AN IRRESISTIBLE VALUE PROPOSITION

EFFECTIVE COMMUNICATION TECHNIQUES

THE POWER OF NETWORKING

CREATING A PERSONALIZED PROSPECTING PLAN

COLD CALLING WITH CONFIDENCE

COLD EMAILING STRATEGIES THAT WORK

USING SOCIAL MEDIA FOR PROSPECTION

TIME MANAGEMENT FOR PROSPECTION

RESPONDING TO OBJECTIONS

FOLLOWING UP WITHOUT BEING INVASIVE

USING CONTENT TO ATTRACT CUSTOMERS

SEO STRATEGIES FOR LEAD GENERATION

DIGITAL TOOLS AND AUTOMATION IN PROSPECTION

CREATING AND MAINTAINING LASTING CUSTOMER RELATIONSHIPS

MEASURING THE SUCCESS OF YOUR PROSPECTION

CREATIVE WAYS TO GENERATE LEADS

SELLING WITHOUT SELLING

NEGOTIATION AND CLOSING SALES

SELF-CARE AND STRESS MANAGEMENT IN SALES

30-DAY ACTION PLAN FOR ACTIVE PROSPECTION

REGINALDO OSNILDO

PRESENTATION

Welcome to a transformative journey that promises to redefine your relationship with active prospecting and sales. If you're reading these words, chances are you're looking for something that can turn the tide in your favor, something that turns difficulties into opportunities and fear into motivation. This is not just another sales book; It is an invitation for you to embark on a less traveled path, where prospecting becomes your greatest ally in the search for success.

Whether you're a solopreneur or the heart of a small business, tackling the challenge of active prospecting can seem like too steep a mountain to climb. The good news? You are not alone. This book, **Fearless Prospecting: How to Win Clients When You Need It Most** , is designed with you in mind, bringing not only a compendium of practical techniques and tested strategies, but also a fresh perspective on how to approach and overcome the barriers that stand between you and your growth.

Through the following pages, I will guide you through a profound transformation, updating traditional prospecting concepts for our time, simplifying processes and, most importantly, helping you build a mindset that will transform the fear of selling into enthusiasm for connecting, engaging and finally conquer.

Each chapter in this book has been carefully designed to complement each other, forming a map that will take you from the fundamentals of active prospecting to the most advanced strategies for maintaining lasting relationships with your clients. You will learn how to identify your target audience, develop an irresistible value proposition, use social media to your advantage, manage your prospecting time effectively, and much more.

This is not just a book; is an interactive learning experience that is intended to be a turning point in your career and life. As you read, you will find invitations to reflect on your own practices and challenges to take you out of your comfort zone that will show you the real power of persistence, innovation, and resilience.

So I invite you to turn the page and start this journey with me. Get ready to unlock the potential of active prospecting, transforming it from a source of stress into a powerful engine to fuel your ambitions, support your family, and grow your business. With each chapter, a new horizon will open, and together, step by step, we will build a bridge over any chasm of doubt or fear, towards the success you deserve and can definitely achieve.

Advance to the next chapter, where we dive deep into **INTRODUCTION TO ACTIVE PROSPECTION**, understanding the essentiality of this skill in your journey to sustainable business growth. Get ready to discover the first step towards fearless prospecting.

Yours sincerely

Reginaldo Osnildo

INTRODUCTION TO ACTIVE PROSPECTION

Active prospecting is the beating heart of any business that seeks not only to survive, but to thrive in an increasingly competitive market. In this chapter, we will unveil the essentiality of active prospecting, understanding how it can become the backbone for sustaining and expanding your customer base, and consequently, your business.

THE FOUNDATION OF BUSINESS SUCCESS

In the business world, the ability to generate new leads and convert those leads into paying customers is what separates successful companies from those struggling to keep the lights on. Active prospecting, in this sense, is much more than a sales tactic; is a business philosophy that places sustainable growth at the center of all business activities.

WHY ACTIVE PROSPECTION?

You may wonder: why focus on active prospecting when there are so many other marketing and sales strategies available? The answer is simple: control and initiative. By mastering the art of active prospecting, you take control of your sales flow. You are not at the mercy of passive marketing campaigns, waiting for potential customers to find you. Instead, you take the initiative, actively seeking out those who will benefit most from what you have to offer.

DEMYSTIFYING PROSPECTION

Many entrepreneurs and salespeople see prospecting as an arduous and often intimidating task. This is often due to a mix of fear of rejection, lack of confidence in one's sales abilities, and a misunderstanding of what prospecting really means. In this book, we will demystify these perceptions, showing that prospecting can be an exciting, rewarding and incredibly effective activity when done correctly.

THE ROLE OF TECHNOLOGY IN MODERN PROSPECTION

In today's sales environment, technology plays a crucial role in active prospecting. Digital tools and automation platforms not only make the process more efficient, but also enable unprecedented personalization and segmentation. This means you can reach the right audience, with the right message, at the right time, significantly increasing your chances of success.

BUILDING RELATIONSHIPS, NOT JUST MAKING SALES

A common misconception about active prospecting is that it focuses exclusively on making a sale. However, the true essence of prospecting is building relationships. Every interaction is an opportunity to better understand your target audience's needs, wants and challenges, allowing you to offer solutions that truly make a difference in their lives or business.

PREPARING FOR THE JOURNEY

As you progress through this chapter, I invite you to approach active prospecting not as a task, but as a journey of discovery. Let's explore techniques, strategies, and mindsets that will not only make this process easier, but also make it more effective and rewarding.

As you close this chapter, I hope you are not only more informed about the critical importance of active prospecting, but also inspired to embrace it as a powerful tool for growth. And with this solid foundation, we're ready to dive even deeper, transforming understanding sales from a daunting task to an exciting activity in the next chapter, **CHANGING YOUR MINDSET ABOUT SALES** . Get ready to transform your mindset and open the doors to sales success like you've never seen before.

CHANGING YOUR MINDSET ABOUT SALES

Selling is an art, a study of human connection, communication and psychology. But why do so many of us shudder at the thought of "making a sale"? This chapter is an invitation to rethink and transform your perception of sales from a daunting task to an exciting journey of personal growth and business success.

SALES: THE MONSTER UNDER THE BED

For many, sales are the monster under the bed. It's that dreaded activity that we conjure up in our minds as something to be avoided at all costs. This fear is often fueled by prejudices about sales being manipulative, forced or invasive. The truth? Sales, at its core, is about creating value and solving problems.

THE SERVICE MENTALITY

The key to transforming your perception of sales starts with a service mindset. When you shift your focus from "I need to sell" to "I have something valuable that can help someone," you begin to see sales in a new light. Selling becomes less about persuading and more about listening, understanding and responding to your customers' needs.

LEARN TO LOVE THE PROCESS

Loving the sales process may seem like a Herculean task at first, but it is absolutely possible. Start by celebrating small victories and learnings, regardless of the outcome. Every "no" is an opportunity to refine your approach, every feedback is a gift to improve. When you focus on the process, not just the result, the sales journey becomes more rewarding.

BUILDING TRUST, INSIDE AND OUT

Trust is the foundation of any successful sales relationship. But to build trust with your customers, you first need to trust yourself and the value you are offering. This starts with a deep understanding of your product or service and a sincere belief in its potential to make a difference.

FACING FEAR HEAD ON

The fear of rejection is, without a doubt, one of the biggest obstacles in selling. However, facing this fear head on is crucial to transforming your sales mindset. Understand that rejection is not personal; It's just part of the process. With every "no" you receive, you are one step closer to a "yes."

SALE AS A JOURNEY OF DISCOVERY

Sales should be seen as a journey of discovery, both for you and your customer. Through the sales process, you have the opportunity to uncover your customers' hidden needs, providing them with solutions they didn't even know they needed. This turns sales from a task into a mission.

Now that we've started to transform your perception of sales, the next step is to identify and deeply understand your target audience. In the next chapter, **IDENTIFICATION OF THE TARGET AUDIENCE**, we will dive into techniques and strategies for finding and understanding your ideal market. Ready to discover where your offers will resonate most strongly and create authentic connections that convert? Advance to the next chapter, where your journey of transformation continues.

IDENTIFICATION OF THE TARGET AUDIENCE

Knowing deeply who your potential customers are is the cornerstone of any effective sales strategy. This chapter is dedicated to uncovering methods for finding and understanding your target audience, ensuring your offerings are not only heard but resonate meaningfully with those who matter most: your future customers.

WHAT IS TARGET AUDIENCE?

Target audience refers to the specific group of people or companies who are most likely to benefit from your products or services. Identifying your target audience is not just knowing who they are, but understanding their needs, desires, pains and how your offer fits into their lives or business.

THE IMPORTANCE OF KNOWING YOUR AUDIENCE

Knowing your target audience is not an academic task; it is a strategic imperative. When you are clear about who you are talking to, your marketing and sales messages become more targeted, personal and effective. This not only increases your chances of conversion but also builds a more engaged and loyal customer base.

STARTING WITH MARKET RESEARCH

The journey to identifying your target audience starts with market research. Utilize online tools, surveys, interviews, and existing market data to gather information about the demographic, behavioral, and psychographic characteristics of your prospects. This information will form the basis for your customer personas, semi-fictional representations of your ideal customer.

CREATING CUSTOMER PERSONAS

Customer personas are incredibly useful tools for visualizing and understanding your target audience. They help humanize demographic and psychographic data, turning them into relatable characters that you and your team can identify with. When developing your personas, include not just demographic information, but also their motivations, challenges, and how they interact with your brand or industry.

DEEPERING INTO YOUR AUDIENCE'S NEEDS

Understanding your target audience requires more than just knowing their basic characteristics; It requires digging deeper into your specific needs and how your product or service can meet those needs. This means actively listening, whether through direct feedback, online behavior analysis or market research. The more you know about what your audience needs and values, the more effective your ability to connect with them will be.

USING FEEDBACK TO REFINE YOUR FOCUS

The target audience identification process is not static; It's a continuous cycle of learning and adjusting. Use feedback from your existing customers to refine your customer personas and approach strategies. This feedback is a treasure trove of insights that can help you fine-tune your offering and messaging in a way that resonates even more deeply with your audience.

With a clear understanding of your target audience, you are now equipped to move forward with confidence. Your marketing and sales strategies can be more focused, personalized and effective, building the foundation for a sustainable and growing business.
In the next chapter, **BUILDING YOUR SALES CONFIDENCE** , we'll explore how you can strengthen your self-confidence and present your offers with conviction, ensuring your audience not only listens, but responds. Get ready to dive deep into yourself, discovering and unlocking the confident salesperson you were born to be.

BUILDING YOUR SALES CONFIDENCE

Trust is the most valuable currency in the sales realm. Not just confidence in your product or service, but more crucially, confidence in yourself as a seller. This chapter is dedicated to strengthening your self-confidence, empowering you to present your offerings with conviction and authenticity. Here, you'll learn strategies for building and displaying unwavering confidence that will attract customers and close sales.

SELF-CONFIDENCE AND ITS ROOTS

Confidence in sales starts with two fundamental beliefs: believing in the value of what you offer and believing in your ability to communicate that value. This means knowing your product or service intimately and recognizing the positive impact it can have on your customers' lives. When you operate from this place of certainty, your confidence naturally soars.

KNOWLEDGE IS POWER

One of the most effective ways to build trust is through in-depth knowledge about your product or service. The more you know, the more prepared you will be to answer questions, resolve concerns, and highlight benefits in a convincing way. Take the time to learn not only the features of your product, but also customer success stories, case studies, and different usage scenarios.

PRACTICE MAKES PERFECTION

Confidence also comes from practice. This means practicing your sales techniques, your sales pitch, and your responses to common objections. The more you practice, especially in a low-stakes environment like role playing with a colleague or mentor, the more natural and confident you will become in real sales situations.

CELEBRATING SMALL VICTORIES

Every small victory is a stepping stone on the path to building your confidence. Celebrate each sale, of course, but also celebrate the steps that lead to it: a good conversation with a prospect, positive feedback, or even a "no" that provided valuable learning. Each of these experiences is a brick in building your confidence.

DEALING WITH REJECTION

Rejection is part of the sales process, but it doesn't have to be a blow to your confidence. See every rejection as an opportunity to learn and grow. Ask yourself: What can I learn from this? Is there feedback I can use to improve? Reframe rejection as a necessary step on the path to success.

BUILDING RELATIONSHIPS, NOT JUST SALES

Remember that sales is, at its core, about building relationships. When you focus on understanding and meeting your customers' needs, rather than simply closing a sale, you create genuine connections. This not only increases your chances of success, but also strengthens your confidence in knowing that you are making a difference.

CONFIDENCE COMES FROM WITHIN

Finally, work on your self-confidence outside of the sales context. This could include mindfulness techniques, affirmation exercises, or simply making time for activities that make you feel good about yourself. When you feel confident in your personal life, that confidence carries over into your professional life.

With your self-confidence strengthened, you're ready to take your sales skills to the next level. In the next chapter, **DEVELOPING AN IRRESISTIBLE VALUE PROPOSITION**, we'll explore how to communicate the value of what you offer in a way that naturally attracts customers to you. Get ready to learn the art of creating and presenting proposals that make clients say "yes."

DEVELOPING AN IRRESISTIBLE VALUE PROPOSITION

At the heart of every successful transaction is a clear, compelling and irresistible value proposition. This chapter is dedicated to helping you develop a value proposition that stands out, effectively communicating the unique value your product or service offers. An irresistible value proposition not only attracts customers, but also convinces them that what you offer is exactly what they need.

UNDERSTANDING VALUE PROPOSITION

A value proposition is a clear promise of the benefit you hope to deliver to your customers. It is the reason why a customer should choose your product or service over your competitors. It should be simple, direct and focused on the real benefits that the customer will experience when making the purchase.

IDENTIFYING CORE VALUE

The first step to developing an irresistible value proposition is identifying the core value of your product or service. Ask yourself: What problem does my product/service solve? How does it improve my clients' lives or businesses? What specific needs does it meet? The core value should be something your target audience truly wants or needs, something that has a meaningful impact for them.

SPEAK YOUR CUSTOMER'S LANGUAGE

For your value proposition to resonate with your target audience, it's crucial to communicate it in their language. This means using words and phrases that they understand and that reflect their wants, needs, and pains. Avoid technical jargon or generic corporate language; be specific, be personal and be relevant.

DIFFERENTIATE YOURSELF FROM THE COMPETITION

One of the key components of an irresistible value proposition is differentiation. What makes your product or service different – and better – than what is available on the market? Focus on your unique selling points and highlight them clearly. Be specific about what you offer that no one else can.

DEMONSTRATE VALUE

It's not enough to just assert your value; you need to demonstrate it. This can be done through case studies, testimonials, performance data or any other evidence that proves the benefits of your product or service. People tend to believe what they see, so providing concrete proof of your value is essential.

SIMPLIFY YOUR MESSAGE

An effective value proposition is simple and straight to the point. Avoid the temptation to include every feature or benefit of your product or service. Focus on what matters most to your customers and present it clearly and concisely. A simple message is more likely to be remembered and understood.

TEST AND REFINE

Developing a value proposition is an iterative process. Test different versions with your target audience to see what resonates best. Ask for feedback and be open to adjusting your proposal based on what you learn. A value proposition can always be improved, so see this process as a journey, not a destination.

With an irresistible value proposition in hand, you are well positioned to capture the attention and interest of your prospects. In the next chapter, **EFFECTIVE COMMUNICATION TECHNIQUES** , we'll delve into how you can improve your communication skills to positively engage and convert these prospects. Be ready to learn the art of communicating in a way that builds relationships, generates trust and drives sales.

EFFECTIVE COMMUNICATION TECHNIQUES

Communicating effectively is key to engaging potential customers and moving them through the sales funnel. This chapter focuses on honing your communication skills, enabling you to authentically connect with your audience and present your value proposition convincingly. Mastering the art of communication not only strengthens your sales, but also builds lasting relationships with your customers.

UNDERSTANDING COMMUNICATION

Communication goes beyond the words you choose; it's about creating a connection. To do this, it is essential to understand not only what you are communicating, but also how your message is received. This involves not only verbal language, but also non-verbal language, such as your posture, gestures and facial expression, as well as the ability to listen actively.

ACTIVE LISTENING

Active listening is one of the most underrated skills in sales. This means listening with the intention to understand, not just to respond. By practicing active listening, you not only show respect for your interlocutor, but you also gain valuable insights into their needs and concerns, which can help you shape your communication more effectively.

ADJUST YOUR MESSAGE

An effective communication technique is the ability to adjust your message based on your audience. This may involve modifying the level of complexity of your language, changing the focus of your message to better align with the listener's needs, or even adapting your communication style to match that of your client. Flexibility in communication shows empathy and increases your ability to connect.

CLARITY AND CONCISION

In communication, less is more. Clear, concise messages

are more easily understood and remembered. Avoid excessive technical jargon and don't overload your client with unnecessary information. Focus on communicating your value proposition directly, highlighting the most relevant benefits for the customer.

THE POWER OF NARRATIVE

Stories have the power to capture attention and connect on an emotional level. By incorporating storytelling – whether recounting customer success stories or sharing a personal experience – you can make your message more relatable and memorable. Stories are also an excellent way to demonstrate the value of your product or service in a tangible way.

NON VERBAL COMUNICATION

Nonverbal communication, such as eye contact, gestures, and tone of voice, plays a crucial role in how your message is received. These elements can reinforce your message, convey trust and help establish a stronger connection. Be aware of your body language and ensure it aligns with what you are saying.

FEEDBACK AS A TOOL

View feedback not as criticism, but as a valuable opportunity to learn and improve. Ask for feedback regularly and use it to refine your communication skills. Be open to adjusting your style based on the responses you receive to better meet your audience's needs.

Mastering effective communication is an essential step towards becoming a successful salesperson. In the next chapter, **THE POWER OF NETWORKING** , we'll explore how you can utilize your existing network to open doors and generate leads. Get ready to learn strategies for significantly expanding your network and how to use those connections to boost your sales success.

THE POWER OF NETWORKING

Networking is not just a business development technique; It's an art that, when done well, can open unimaginable doors, generate valuable leads and establish lasting partnerships. This chapter dives into effective networking strategies, helping you utilize your existing network and expand it in ways that support and accelerate your prospecting efforts.

UNDERSTANDING NETWORKING

Networking goes beyond collecting business cards; It's about building genuine, trusting relationships. Every person you meet has the potential to become a customer, a partner, or even a promoter of your business. The key is to approach networking with the right mindset, focusing on how you can add value to others, rather than just what you can gain.

START WITH YOUR EXISTING NETWORK

Your current network is the perfect starting point. Consider family, friends, past coworkers, clients, and even casual acquaintances. Take inventory of the people you already know and identify how they might fit into your networking strategy. A pre-existing personal connection can be a powerful avenue for introductions and recommendations.

STRATEGIES TO EXPAND YOUR NETWORK

- **Networking events:** Attending industry-specific or local networking events is an excellent way to meet new people. Come prepared with a brief and memorable introduction about yourself and your business.

- **Professional groups and associations:** Join groups relevant to your industry, both online and offline. These are great places to meet people with similar interests and challenges.

- **Social media platforms:** LinkedIn, Twitter, and industry-specific Facebook groups can be powerful tools for connecting with professionals in your field. Share valuable content and engage in conversations to increase your visibility.

- **Volunteering:** Volunteering your time or skills to causes or organizations can be a way to not only contribute to your community, but also meet people with similar values.

BUILDING LONG-TERM RELATIONSHIPS

Effective networking is about nurturing relationships, not just making initial contact. Stay in touch with your network through regular messages, sharing articles of interest, or even arranging casual meetings. Remember that reciprocity is fundamental; look for ways to help or add value to others whenever possible.

DIGITAL NETWORKING

In an increasingly digital world, your online presence is as important as your physical presence. Keep your social media profiles up to date and professional. Use these platforms to highlight your knowledge, share successes, and contribute to relevant discussions. Additionally, consider creating your own content to increase your authority and visibility in the industry.

THE NETWORKING ETIQUETTE

- **Be authentic:** People are attracted to authenticity. Be yourself and show genuine interest in others.

- **Listen more than you talk:** Listening carefully shows respect and allows you to better understand the other person's needs and interests.

- **Follow through:** If you promised to send information, give an introduction, or share resources, make sure you follow through. This builds trust and credibility.

With these networking strategies in hand, you are well-equipped to build and cultivate a network of contacts that not only supports your active prospecting goals, but also enriches your entrepreneurial journey in ways you might not have imagined. In the next chapter, **CREATING A PERSONALIZED PROSPECTING PLAN**, we'll dive into the tactics for creating a tailored action plan that leverages your strengths and maximizes your prospecting efforts. Get ready to transform your networking into concrete results.

CREATING A PERSONALIZED PROSPECTING PLAN

After establishing a solid foundation of knowledge about your target audience, building your sales confidence, developing an irresistible value proposition, improving your communication techniques and expanding your network, the next step is to create a personalized prospecting plan. This chapter will guide you through building a strategic plan that leverages your strengths, fits your personality, and maximizes your prospecting efforts for exceptional results.

DEFINING YOUR PROSPECTING OBJECTIVES

Start with the end in mind. Set clear and measurable objectives for your prospecting. This may include goals related to the number of new leads generated, lead-to-customer conversion rates, or increased revenue. Having specific goals allows you to create a targeted plan and measure your success effectively.

KNOWING YOUR STRENGTHS

Each person has a unique set of skills and preferences. Some may excel at face-to-face communication, while others may be masters at persuasive writing. Assess your strengths and consider how you can utilize them most effectively in your prospecting plan. For example, if you are exceptional at written communication, techniques like cold emailing may be a better fit for you.

CHOOSING YOUR PROSPECTING TACTICS

Based on your strengths and goals, select the prospecting tactics that best align with your profile and target market. This can range from networking and attending events to digital prospecting such as SEO or content marketing. Remember, quality is more important than quantity; It's better to choose a few tactics that you can execute well than to try to do everything averagely.

CREATING A PROSPECTING SCHEDULE

Consistency is key to successful prospecting. Create a detailed schedule, including when and how often you will carry out your prospecting activities. This can help turn prospecting from a sporadic task into an integrated part of your daily or weekly routine. Make sure you also allocate time for regular analysis and adjustments to the plan.

AUTOMATING AND DELEGATING WHEN POSSIBLE

Look for ways to make your prospecting process more efficient. Automation tools can help with tasks like scheduling emails, posting to social media, and tracking customer interactions. Delegating specific tasks to team members or freelancers can also free up your time to focus on prospecting activities that require your personal touch.

MONITORING AND ADJUSTING YOUR PLAN

A prospecting plan is a living document; it should be regularly reviewed and adjusted based on performance and feedback received. Set regular intervals to evaluate the success of your prospecting tactics and make necessary changes. Remember, flexibility to adapt is a competitive advantage.

Creating a personalized prospecting plan is a key step in transforming active prospecting from a source of stress into an exciting growth strategy. By aligning this plan with your goals, strengths, and preferences, you lay a solid foundation for sustainable sales success.

Ready to put your plan into action? In the next chapter, **COLD CALLING WITH CONFIDENCE**, we'll explore how to approach one of the most traditional and challenging prospecting techniques with a new perspective and renewed confidence. Be prepared to turn the dreaded cold call into a powerful tool in your prospecting arsenal.

COLD CALLING WITH CONFIDENCE

Cold calling, the practice of calling potential customers without prior contact, is often seen as one of the most challenging tasks in sales. However, with the right approach and a healthy dose of confidence, cold calling can turn into an effective and even rewarding strategy. This chapter is designed to equip you with techniques and mindsets that will transform your cold calls from sources of anxiety to opportunities for growth.

DEMYSTIFYING COLD CALLING

The first step to approaching cold calling with confidence is changing your perception of it. Cold calling is not about interruption or inconvenience; It's an opportunity for you to present a solution that can genuinely benefit your potential customer. Treat each call as a service, not a forced sale.

PREPARATION IS THE KEY

Solid preparation is essential to cold calling success. This means researching the company and person you are calling, understanding their challenges and needs. Create a basic script for your call, but be prepared to deviate from it; the roadmap should serve as a guide, not a rigid script.

BUILDING RAPPORT QUICKLY

In the first few moments of a cold call, it's crucial to establish a connection. This can be done by mentioning something you have in common, making an observation about something recent in the potential client's industry, or simply being friendly and approachable. Rapport is the foundation for trust and openness during conversation.

FOCUSING ON BENEFITS, NOT FEATURES

During your call, focus on how your product or service can benefit the customer. Avoid the temptation to list all the features; instead, highlight how these characteristics solve specific problems or improve situations for your potential customer. This makes the conversation more relevant and engaging for them.

DEALING WITH OBJECTIONS

Objections are a natural part of the cold calling process. Instead of dreading them, see them as opportunities to better understand your potential customer's concerns and respond in a polite and informative way. The key here is to actively listen, validate the customer's concern, and then present information that can help overcome the objection.

MAINTAINING A POSITIVE ATTITUDE

A positive attitude is contagious and can make a big difference in how receptive your call is. Even when faced with rejection, maintain a friendly and professional tone. Every call is an opportunity to hone your skills, so try to learn from the experience, regardless of the outcome.

PRACTICING AND IMPROVING

Like many skills, cold calling improves with practice. Don't be discouraged by rejections or difficult calls; instead, use them as feedback to refine your approach. Also consider seeking feedback from peers or mentors who can offer valuable perspectives and tips.

Cold calling doesn't have to be a dreaded task. With the right preparation, a positive mindset, and a genuine focus on how you can help your prospects, you can turn cold calls into productive conversations and, eventually, valuable business relationships.

As we move forward, the next chapter, **COLD EMAILING STRATEGIES THAT WORK**, will explore how to complement your cold calling techniques with effective cold emailing strategies, ensuring a comprehensive, multi-faceted prospecting approach. Get ready to master another vital tool in your prospecting arsenal.

COLD EMAILING STRATEGIES THAT WORK

Cold emailing, like cold calling, is a powerful prospecting tool when used correctly. However, with potential customers' inboxes often saturated, getting your email not only opened, but also read and responded to requires a strategic and personalized approach. This chapter will guide you through effective cold emailing strategies, allowing you to create emails that stand out and drive results.

THE IMPORTANCE OF THE SUBJECT LINE

The subject line is, without a doubt, the most critical element of your cold email. It's the first point of contact and the main factor that determines whether your email will be opened. Subject lines should be clear, intriguing, and personalized, giving the recipient a reason to click. Avoid words that sound like spam and opt for phrases that spark curiosity or highlight a clear benefit.

CUSTOMIZATION IS THE KEY

Sending the same generic email to all your contacts is a recipe for failure. Personalization shows that you took the time to get to know the recipient and their company, increasing the chances of engagement. Use the recipient's name, reference recent company projects, or mention specific industry challenges to create an immediate connection.

FOCUS ON VALUE, NOT SALES

The objective of your cold email should not be to sell from the first line, but rather to start a conversation. Focus on how you can add value to the recipient or help solve a specific problem they may be facing. By positioning yourself as a valuable resource rather than just another salesperson, you increase the chances of a positive response.

CLARITY AND CONCISION

An effective cold email gets straight to the point. Keep your message short, clear and focused on the value you are offering.

Each sentence should have a purpose, whether it's capturing attention, highlighting a benefit or calling to action. Remember, your recipient's time is precious, so make it count.

CLEAR CALL TO ACTION

Your email should end with a clear and specific call to action (CTA). This could be a request for a meeting, a response to a specific question, or an offer to send more information. Whatever the CTA, it should be simple and require minimal effort on the part of the recipient to increase your chances of engagement.

STRATEGIC FOLLOW-UP

Follow-up is a crucial part of the cold emailing process. If you don't hear back, send a follow-up email after a few days, gently reminding the recipient about your previous message and reinforcing the value you can offer. Limiting yourself to one or two follow-up emails is generally considered good practice to avoid being intrusive.

TESTING AND OPTIMIZATION

Just like other forms of marketing, cold emailing is an iterative process. Test different subject lines, message styles, and calls to action to see what generates the best response. Use open, click, and response rates to refine your approach over time.

Cold emailing, when done correctly, can be an exceptionally effective prospecting strategy. With a personalized, value-focused and clear approach, your emails will not only be read, but also act as a starting point for valuable business relationships.

Moving on, the next chapter, **USING SOCIAL MEDIA FOR PROSPECTION**, will explore how you can leverage social media platforms to identify and engage potential customers, complementing your cold calling and emailing strategies with success on social media. Get ready to expand your reach and strengthen your prospecting strategies with the power of social media.

USING SOCIAL MEDIA FOR PROSPECTION

Social media has transformed the way we connect, communicate and even do business. For sales professionals and small business owners, they offer a dynamic platform for prospecting, allowing you to reach potential customers where they are already active. This chapter focuses on effective strategies for using social media in prospecting, helping you identify, engage and convert potential customers in a digital environment.

CHOOSING THE RIGHT PLATFORMS

The first step is to identify which social media platforms your potential customers are most active on. While LinkedIn is often the default choice for B2B prospecting, platforms like Twitter, Facebook and Instagram can be equally valuable depending on your target market. The key is to focus your efforts on the platforms that offer the greatest return on your investment of time and resources.

BUILDING AN ATTRACTIVE PROFILE

Before you start prospecting, it's crucial that your own social media profile is optimized and professional. This means having a clear profile photo, a well-written bio that highlights your value and experience, and, if applicable, a portfolio of past work or testimonials. Your profile should communicate not only who you are, but how you can help your potential customers.

AUTHENTIC ENGAGEMENT

The secret to effective social media prospecting is authentic engagement. This could include sharing relevant content, commenting on potential clients' posts, or participating in discussions in industry groups. The goal is to build genuine relationships, providing value and establishing yourself as an authority in your field, not just selling your product or service.

CONTENT STRATEGIES

Creating and sharing content that is both informative and

engaging is a powerful way to attract potential customers. This can range from blog articles and case studies to videos and infographics. Content not only helps establish your expertise, but it also provides a reason for potential clients to connect and interact with you.

MONITORING AND INTERACTING

Use social media monitoring tools to track mentions of your brand, products, services, or industry-relevant keywords. This not only helps you identify prospecting opportunities, but also allows you to proactively interact with potential customers by answering questions, offering solutions, or simply thanking them for mentions or shares.

TAKING ADVANTAGE OF PAID ADVERTISING

Social media platforms offer robust paid advertising options that can be used to specifically target your target audience with personalized messages. Whether through LinkedIn ads to reach professionals in a certain industry or Facebook campaigns to reach an audience with specific interests, paid ads can be an efficient way to increase your reach and generate qualified leads.

MEASURING YOUR SUCCESS

As with all sales and marketing strategies, measurement is essential to understand what is working and what needs to be adjusted. Use analytics tools provided by social media platforms to track engagement, audience growth, and lead conversion. This data will provide valuable insights to optimize your prospecting approach.

Social media prospecting, when done correctly, can be an effective way to build relationships and generate leads. By combining an optimized profile, authentic engagement, valuable content and proactive monitoring, you can transform social media into a powerful channel for growing your business.

Moving forward, the next chapter, **TIME MANAGEMENT FOR PROSPECTION**, will cover how to organize your schedule to maximize the time dedicated to prospecting, ensuring that you can effectively balance this essential activity with other responsibilities of your business. Get ready to learn how to manage your time in a way that enhances your prospecting strategies.

TIME MANAGEMENT FOR PROSPECTION

Prospecting is a crucial activity that feeds the sales funnel and sustains business growth. However, without effective time management, you can easily fall into the trap of putting prospecting aside in favor of more immediate or comfortable tasks. This chapter focuses on time management strategies that ensure adequate allocation of resources for prospecting while balancing it with other important daily responsibilities.

ESTABLISHING PRIORITIES

Start by identifying prospecting as one of your top priorities. This means consciously recognizing the value of prospecting to the long-term success of your business and committing to dedicating regular time to this activity. Remember, prospecting is not just an additional task; It is the engine that drives growth.

DEDICATED TIME BLOCKS

An effective time management technique is to use blocks of time dedicated exclusively to prospecting. This could be a few hours a day or specific blocks of time throughout the week. During these times, minimize distractions and focus fully on prospecting activities. Regularity and consistency are key to turning prospecting into a productive habit.

AUTOMATION AND TOOLS

Technology can be a great ally in saving time during the prospecting process. Use automation tools for repetitive tasks, like sending follow-up emails or posting to social media. Additionally, use CRMs (Customer Relationship Management) to organize leads, monitor interactions and schedule reminders for follow-ups.

GROUPED TASKS

Grouping similar tasks together can significantly increase efficiency. Dedicate blocks of time to specific activities, such as researching potential customers, sending emails , making phone calls or updating your CRM. This helps you stay focused and reduce time wasted transitioning between different types of tasks.

DELEGATION

Consider delegating activities that don't require your direct attention. This could include initial lead qualification, social media profile management, or even market research. Delegating tasks to team members or virtual assistants can free up your time to focus on high-value prospecting activities.

SETTING CLEAR GOALS

Set clear, measurable goals for your prospecting activities. This could include a specific number of new contacts per week, a number of prospecting emails sent, or a number of cold calls made. Goals help you stay focused and give you a clear yardstick for evaluating your progress.

REVIEW AND ADJUSTMENT

Regularly review your time management and prospecting activities. This involves analyzing what's working, what's not, and adjusting your approach as needed. Adaptability is crucial as it allows you to optimize your effectiveness and ensure that your time is always well invested.

Effective time management in prospecting not only ensures that this crucial activity receives the attention it deserves, but also maximizes the effectiveness of your efforts. By implementing solid time management strategies, you can ensure that prospecting takes its rightful place as an unwavering priority in your day-to-day business.

Moving on, the next chapter, **RESPONDING TO OBJECTIONS**, will dive into strategies for turning objections into opportunities, helping you overcome barriers and advance sales conversations. Be prepared to approach objections not as obstacles, but as stepping stones to sales success.

RESPONDING TO OBJECTIONS

Facing objections is a natural part of the sales process. Instead of seeing them as barriers to success, you can transform them into opportunities to deepen your understanding of customer needs and reinforce the value of your offer. This chapter explores strategies for responding to objections effectively, helping you navigate these critical moments and move through the sales conversation with confidence.

UNDERSTANDING THE OBJECTIONS

The first step to effectively responding to an objection is to understand its origin. Objections often arise from a lack of information or understanding, concerns about cost or value, or simply resistance to change. Listening carefully and asking clarifying questions can help you identify the root of the objection and address it in a targeted way.

VIEWING OBJECTIONS AS OPPORTUNITIES

Each objection provides an opportunity to learn more about what your potential customer values or cares about. Additionally, approaching objections in a positive and constructive way can strengthen trust by demonstrating that you are genuinely interested in finding the best solution to their needs.

STRUCTURE FOR ANSWERING OBJECTIONS

An effective framework for responding to objections follows four main steps:

- **Listen:** Give the customer the opportunity to fully express their objection without interruptions.

- **Clarify:** Ask questions to fully understand the objection. This also shows that you are listening and care about their concerns.

- **Respond:** Address the objection directly, providing information, examples, and testimony that can help mitigate the concern.

- **Confirm:** Check whether your response satisfies the customer's objection and whether there are any further questions.

CUSTOMIZE YOUR RESPONSE

While it's helpful to have prepared responses to common objections, personalization is crucial. Use what you know about the customer's specific needs and wants to shape your response. This not only makes your answer more relevant, but also demonstrates a commitment to providing a truly personalized solution.

VALUE-BASED RESPONSES

When customers express concerns about price, it's an opportunity to reinforce the value of your product or service. Explain how the benefits outweigh the cost and how the offer could save time, money, or other resources in the long run. Success stories from similar customers can be particularly persuasive in this context.

PRACTICE AND PREPARE

Practice leads to perfection. Gather common objections in your industry and practice your responses. Not only will this help you feel more confident during sales conversations, but it will also ensure your responses are coherent, informative, and convincing.

KEEP THE CONVERSATION GOING

Finally, after addressing an objection, it's important to redirect the conversation back to the sales path. Ask an open-ended question that allows the customer to express any other concerns or return to the dialogue about the benefits and advantages of your offering.

Responding to objections is not an obstacle, but an integral part of the sales process that, when handled correctly, can bring you closer to closing the sale. View each objection as a chance to deepen your customer relationship and solidify their trust in your offering.

As we move forward, the next chapter, **FOLLOWING UP WITHOUT BEING INVASIVE** , will focus on how to balance persistence and courtesy when following up with prospects, ensuring you maintain the connection without overstepping boundaries. Get ready to learn the art of moving forward respectfully and effectively.

FOLLOWING UP WITHOUT BEING INVASIVE

Follow-up is a crucial step in the sales process, but finding the right balance without becoming intrusive can be challenging. This chapter covers effective strategies for maintaining interest and advancing the conversation with potential customers, respecting their limits and time.

THE IMPORTANCE OF TIMING

Timing is everything when it comes to moving forward. Taking too long to get in touch can cause the lead to cool off, but being too quick can feel like sales pressure. The key is to establish a reasonable timeline based on customer leads and industry norms. After the first contact or presentation, leaving a few days space before the first follow-up can be a good starting point.

CUSTOMIZE YOUR FOLLOW-UPS

Each interaction with a potential customer should be personalized to reflect previous conversations, their specific interests, and any objections that have been raised. This demonstrates that you are attentive to their needs and concerns, and not just sending generic messages. Personalization increases the relevance of your follow-up and the likelihood of a positive response.

PROVIDE VALUE IN EVERY INTERACTION

Each follow-up should offer additional value to the potential customer. This could be in the form of industry insights, relevant articles, case studies, or demonstrations of how your product or service can solve a specific problem they face. Continuously providing value reinforces the perception that you are interested in helping, not just selling.

USE MULTIPLE COMMUNICATION CHANNELS

Diversifying communication channels can help keep follow-up fresh and less intrusive. In addition to email, consider using phone calls, LinkedIn messages, or even handwritten notes, depending on the customer relationship and preferences. The important thing is to respect the customer's preferences on how they would like to be contacted.

THE ART OF ASKING

Encourage dialogue by asking open-ended questions in your follow-ups. Not only does this provide the customer with an easy opportunity to respond, but it can also reveal valuable information about their hesitations or needs. Questions such as "Is there any additional information I can provide to help with your decision?" invite interaction without pressure.

KNOW WHEN TO BACK OFF

Recognizing when to stop insisting is just as important as knowing when to move on. If a potential client clearly expresses that they are not interested or asks not to be contacted again, respect their request. Maintaining a professional and courteous demeanor leaves the door open for future interactions should circumstances change.

MONITORING AND ADJUSTING YOUR APPROACH

Tracking your response rates and adjusting your follow-up strategies based on what works is key. Take note of which approaches generate the most engagement and be willing to try new techniques to improve their effectiveness.

Moving forward without being intrusive is a delicate balance that requires attention to detail, personalization, and respect for the client's preferences and boundaries. By implementing the strategies above, you can maintain effective communication that advances the sale without compromising the customer relationship.

Moving on, the next chapter, **USING CONTENT TO ATTRACT CUSTOMERS** , will dive into the creation and strategic use of content to support your prospecting efforts, attracting prospects through demonstrating value and knowledge. Get ready to explore how content marketing can be a powerful tool in your sales arsenal.

USING CONTENT TO ATTRACT CUSTOMERS

In today's sales and marketing landscape, content plays a key role in attracting and engaging potential customers. By offering valuable and relevant information, you not only establish your brand as an authority in the industry, but you also create a path for potential customers to come to you. This chapter explores how to strategically use content to support your prospecting efforts and attract customers.

DEFINING YOUR CONTENT STRATEGY

Before you start creating content, it's important to define a clear strategy. This includes understanding your target audience, identifying the topics that are most relevant to them, and determining the best channels to distribute your content. Your content strategy should align with your prospecting and sales goals, aiming to solve problems or answer questions that your prospects may have.

TYPES OF CONTENT TO ATTRACT CUSTOMERS

- **Blog posts:** Informative articles that cover topics relevant to your audience can help improve your visibility in search engines and establish your brand as a valuable resource.

- **E-books and whitepapers:** Longer, more detailed content can be used to generate leads by asking visitors to provide their contact information in exchange for the download.

- **Videos:** Explainer videos, customer testimonials, and product overviews are highly engaging and can be shared easily on social media.

- **Infographics:** Complex information presented in a visual and accessible way can help capture attention and facilitate sharing online.

- **Webinars:** Online educational sessions can be an excellent way to demonstrate your expertise and interact directly with potential customers.

PROMOTING YOUR CONTENT

Creating valuable content is only half the battle; promoting it effectively is equally important. Use social media, emails, SEO and even partnerships with influencers or other brands to expand the reach of your content. Cross-promotion between different channels can significantly increase visibility and engagement.

MEASURING CONTENT SUCCESS

To understand the impact of your content, it's crucial to track metrics like website traffic, social media engagement, asset downloads, and most importantly, lead conversions. This information will help you refine your content strategy and focus on the types of content that drive the best results.

CONTENT AS A PROSPECTION TOOL

In addition to attracting potential customers, content can be actively used in prospecting. Including links to relevant content in cold emails or social media messages can add value to your communication and increase response rates. Content can also be a great starting point for discussions during sales calls or meetings.

BUILDING RELATIONSHIPS THROUGH CONTENT

Finally, content is not just a tool for attracting customers, but also for building and nurturing relationships with them. By providing consistent, valuable content, you keep your brand in customers' minds and establish a foundation of trust that can lead to lasting business relationships.

Strategically using content to attract customers is a powerful approach in the digital age. By creating and promoting content that resonates with your target audience, you can not only increase your visibility and authority, but also generate qualified leads and establish meaningful relationships with potential customers.

Moving forward, the next chapter, **SEO STRATEGIES FOR LEAD GENERATION** , will dive into how to optimize your online presence to be found by potential customers, ensuring your content and brand reach the right audience at the right time. Get ready to explore the power of SEO in your prospecting strategy.

SEO STRATEGIES FOR LEAD GENERATION

Search engine optimization (SEO) is a powerful tool for improving your brand's online visibility and attracting potential customers organically. The key to an effective SEO strategy is ensuring that your content and website are found by potential customers when they are searching for the solutions you offer. This chapter explores fundamental SEO strategies to improve your lead generation.

UNDERSTANDING SEO

SEO involves a series of practices designed to improve your website's position in search results for relevant terms and phrases. This is achieved by optimizing various elements of your website, including content, structure, meta tags, internal and external links, among others. The goal is to make your website more attractive to search engines and users.

KEYWORD RESEARCH

The first step in any SEO strategy is keyword research. This involves identifying the terms your target audience uses when searching for information, products or services related to your business. Tools like Google Keyword Planner and SEMrush can help you identify these keywords, as well as the search volume and competition for them.

ON-PAGE OPTIMIZATION

Once you have identified your target keywords, the next step is to integrate them into your website. This includes optimizing titles, meta descriptions, headers, and the page content itself to include your keywords in a natural and relevant way. Additionally, ensure that your website has a logical structure that is easy to navigate for both users and search engines.

QUALITY CONTENT

Content is the heart of SEO. Producing original, valuable and relevant content not only attracts visitors to your website, but also encourages other websites to link to yours, which can significantly improve your search engine rankings. Blogs, case studies, e-books, infographics, and videos are all content formats that can be optimized for SEO.

TECHNICAL SEO

Technical SEO refers to optimizing your website's infrastructure to ensure it is indexed and ranked effectively by search engines. This includes improving site speed, ensuring your site is mobile-friendly, using SSL, optimizing URLs, and creating a sitemap.xml file to help search engines crawl your site more easily.

LINK BUILDING

Building a strong backlink profile is another crucial component of SEO. This involves getting links from other authority sites to yours. Strategies to achieve this include creating shareable content, guest blogging, and participating in relevant business directories. Quality links tell search engines that your site is a reliable source of information.

MEASUREMENT AND ADJUSTMENT

Finally, it's crucial to monitor your website's performance on search engines and adjust your strategy as needed. Tools like Google Analytics and Google Search Console can provide valuable insights into website traffic, conversions, and the performance of your keywords, allowing you to continually refine your SEO approach to improve lead generation.

A well-executed SEO strategy can significantly increase your website's visibility, attract qualified traffic, and generate leads organically. By focusing on keyword research, on-page optimization, quality content, technical SEO, and link building, you can improve your search engine rankings and capture the attention of potential customers at the right time.

Moving forward, the next chapter, **DIGITAL TOOLS AND**

AUTOMATION IN PROSPECTION , will explore how technology can simplify and make your prospecting strategies more efficient, allowing you to focus on building relationships and closing sales. Get ready to discover tools that can transform your prospecting approach.

DIGITAL TOOLS AND AUTOMATION IN PROSPECTION

In today's digital world, technology offers a multitude of tools that can streamline and automate many aspects of prospecting, making the process more efficient and allowing you to spend more time on meaningful human interaction. This chapter explores digital tools and automation in prospecting, highlighting how they can transform your prospecting strategies.

CRM (CUSTOMER RELATIONSHIP MANAGEMENT)

CRM systems are the heart of digital prospecting, allowing you to organize, track and manage leads and customers throughout the sales cycle. They provide a 360-degree view of your customer interactions, purchase history, preferences and more, making it easy to personalize your sales approach and identify upsell and cross-sell opportunities.

EMAIL AUTOMATION

Email automation allows you to send personalized emails to segmented lists of contacts based on specific actions, such as visiting a page on your website, downloading a resource, or abandoning a shopping cart. Lead nurturing campaigns can be automated to deliver relevant content at scheduled intervals, moving leads through the sales funnel efficiently.

PROSPECTING AND RESEARCH TOOLS

There are several tools available specifically designed to help identify and research potential customers. These tools can provide valuable information such as contact details, company size, industry and even buying signals, allowing you to personalize your prospecting approach and direct efforts towards the most promising leads.

SCHEDULING AUTOMATION

Automated scheduling tools like Calendly or HubSpot Meetings allow potential clients to schedule meetings or calls with you without the need for endless email exchanges. These tools can be integrated into your calendar, showing your real-time availability and automating meeting reminders, improving the customer experience and saving time.

SOCIAL SELLING AND MONITORING TOOLS

Social selling is an important strategy in modern prospecting. Social media monitoring tools allow you to track your brand mentions, relevant keywords, and competitor activity. Additionally, platforms like LinkedIn Sales Navigator are designed to help with B2B prospecting by offering advanced search features and personalized lead recommendations.

ANALYSIS AND REPORTS

Analytics and reporting tools provide valuable insights into the performance of your prospecting strategies, from the effectiveness of email campaigns to social media engagement and website conversions. This data allows you to adjust your tactics in real time, focusing efforts on the activities that generate the best results.

PRIVACY AND COMPLIANCE CONSIDERATIONS

When implementing digital tools and automation, it is vital to consider privacy and compliance issues, especially in relation to regulations such as GDPR. Ensure your practices are compliant and that customer data privacy is always prioritized.

Digital tools and automation in prospecting are not just about efficiency; they are about improving the quality of interactions with prospects and personalizing the sales journey to their specific needs. By adopting these technologies, you can transform your prospecting approach, creating more sales opportunities and building stronger customer relationships.

The next chapter, **CREATING AND MAINTAINING LASTING CUSTOMER RELATIONSHIPS** , will delve deeper into how to nurture these initial contacts into lasting, profitable relationships, utilizing the tools and strategies discussed to maximize long-term customer value. Get ready to discover the secret to turning leads into loyal customers.

CREATING AND MAINTAINING LASTING CUSTOMER RELATIONSHIPS

Building lasting relationships with customers goes beyond sales conversion. It's about cultivating trust, offering ongoing value, and creating a positive experience that encourages long-term customer loyalty. This chapter focuses on effective strategies for not only gaining new customers, but keeping those relationships growing and thriving over time.

KNOWING YOUR CUSTOMERS

A lasting relationship starts with a deep understanding of who your customers are, their needs, wants, challenges and how your products or services fit into their lives. Use data collected during the sales process, direct feedback, and interactions to create detailed customer profiles, allowing you to personalize your communications and offers.

CONSISTENT AND PERSONALIZED COMMUNICATION

Maintain regular communication with your customers, but ensure that each interaction brings value. Use the data collected to personalize your messages, whether through personalized emails, exclusive offers or relevant content. Remember, personalization is key to making customers feel valued and understood.

PROVIDE EXCEPTIONAL SUPPORT

Excellent customer service is critical to maintaining lasting relationships. This means not only resolving issues quickly, but also exceeding expectations whenever possible. Provide multiple support channels, train your team to be empathetic and helpful, and always seek feedback to improve.

REWARD LOYALTY

Loyalty and rewards programs can be an effective way to encourage and thank customers for their continued patronage. Exclusive offers, discounts, early access to new products or services, and recognition on social media platforms are all ways to show appreciation and reinforce customer loyalty.

INVOLVE CUSTOMERS IN PRODUCT EVOLUTION

Customers feel more engaged and valued when they have a say in the development of products or services. Consider implementing customer feedback programs or focus groups to gather insights that can guide innovations or improvements. Communicating how customer feedback contributed to changes can also strengthen the relationship.

AFTER-SALES FOLLOW-UP

The customer relationship does not end with the sale. After-sales follow-ups to check customer satisfaction and provide additional support can turn a one-time sale into an ongoing relationship. This can also be an opportunity to collect valuable feedback and identify opportunities for upselling or cross-selling .

BUILD A COMMUNITY

Creating a community around your brand can foster a sense of belonging among your customers. This can be done through online forums, social media groups, or customer-only events. An active community not only supports existing customers, but can also attract new customers through referrals and recommendations.

BE PRESENT AND AVAILABLE

Finally, being present and accessible to your customers communicates that you value the relationship. Be responsive on social media, offer direct communication channels and be available to talk and resolve any issues that arise.

Creating and maintaining lasting customer relationships is an ongoing investment in the long-term success of your business. By focusing on getting to know your customers, personalizing communication, providing exceptional support, and involving them in your brand journey, you can build a loyal customer base who will not only continue to buy from you, but also become advocates for your brand.

Moving on, the next chapter, **MEASURING THE SUCCESS OF YOUR PROSPECTION**, will detail how to identify and use key performance indicators (KPIs) to evaluate and refine your prospecting and customer relationship strategies, ensuring your efforts are aligned with growth objectives of your business. Get ready to learn how to measure the success of your initiatives effectively.

MEASURING THE SUCCESS OF YOUR PROSPECTION

To ensure that your prospecting and customer relationship strategies are effective and contributing to the growth of your business, it is crucial to measure the success of these initiatives. This chapter discusses how to identify, monitor, and use key performance indicators (KPIs) to evaluate the effectiveness of your prospecting techniques and adjust your strategies as needed.

ESTABLISHING PROSPECTION KPIS

Prospecting KPIs should be aligned with your business's overall sales and marketing objectives. Some fundamental KPIs include:

- **Lead conversion rate:** The percentage of leads that convert into paying customers. This indicator can help you evaluate the quality of leads generated by your prospecting activities.

- **Cost per lead (CPL):** The total cost of generating leads divided by the total number of leads. This KPI is crucial for evaluating the efficiency of your marketing and prospecting efforts.

- **Response rate:** The percentage of contacts who respond to your prospecting attempts, such as emails or calls. A low response rate may indicate a need to adjust your message or approach.

- **Time to close:** The average time needed to convert a lead into a customer. This KPI can help identify bottlenecks in the sales process.

- **Customer Lifecycle Value (CLV):** The total revenue expected from a customer over the course of their relationship with the company. This indicator highlights the importance of maintaining lasting relationships with customers.

MONITORING AND ANALYZING DATA

With the KPIs established, the next step is to implement systems to collect and analyze this data. CRM tools, marketing automation, and web analytics platforms can provide valuable insights into the performance of your prospecting activities. Monitor these KPIs regularly to identify trends, successes and areas that require attention.

ADJUSTING DATA-BASED STRATEGIES

Analyzing KPIs can reveal crucial insights that allow you to adjust your prospecting strategies to improve performance. For example, if your lead conversion rate is low, it may indicate a need to review your target audience or value proposition. If your CPL is high, explore ways to optimize your marketing campaigns to reduce costs.

A/B TESTS

Implementing A/B testing into your prospecting campaigns can help you determine which strategies, messages, or channels are most effective. Compare different approaches to see which one generates better results in terms of conversion, response and engagement rates.

LISTENING TO CUSTOMER FEEDBACK

In addition to quantitative KPIs, qualitative customer feedback is a rich source of insights. Customer satisfaction surveys, post-sale feedback and reviews can provide valuable insights into how to improve your prospecting approach and strengthen customer relationships.

Measuring the success of your prospecting is essential to understanding the impact of your strategies on business growth. By establishing clear KPIs, regularly monitoring performance, and adjusting your tactics based on hard data and customer feedback, you can optimize your prospecting activities to achieve better, more sustainable results.

As we move forward, the next chapter, **CREATIVE WAYS TO GENERATE LEADS** , will explore innovative strategies for identifying and capturing leads, encouraging you to think outside the box in your own prospecting initiatives. Get ready to discover unique approaches that can differentiate your business and attract more potential customers.

CREATIVE WAYS TO GENERATE LEADS

Lead generation is the engine that drives business growth, but in an increasingly saturated market, standing out from the competition requires creativity and innovation. This chapter presents unconventional and creative strategies for generating leads, encouraging you to explore new approaches to attracting potential customers.

GAMIFICATION FOR ENGAGEMENT

Incorporating gaming elements into your marketing strategy can significantly increase engagement and capture lead information in a fun way. For example, creating an interactive quiz related to your industry, where participants provide their email to see the results, can be an effective way to generate qualified leads while offering value.

PARTNERSHIPS WITH NICHE INFLUENCERS

Collaborating with influencers who have a similar target audience to yours can open your business to a completely new customer base. The key is to choose influencers whose values and audience align well with your brand, ensuring the partnership is authentic and appealing to both audiences.

THEMED VIRTUAL EVENTS

Hosting virtual events like webinars, workshops, or even themed virtual happy hours can be an excellent way to generate interest and collect lead information. These events not only position your brand as a thought leader in your industry, but they also create an environment conducive to direct interaction with potential customers.

COMPETITIONS AND SWEEPSTAKES ON SOCIAL MEDIA

Contests and sweepstakes are proven techniques for generating engagement and capturing leads. By asking participants to follow your pages, share your content, or tag friends, you not only expand your reach but also collect valuable contact data for future marketing campaigns.

EXCLUSIVE OFFERS FOR FOLLOWERS

Creating exclusive offers for your social media followers or newsletter subscribers can motivate sharing and sign-ups, generating new leads. Whether it's a special discount, early access to products, or exclusive content, these offers encourage action and reinforce brand loyalty.

INTERACTIVE CONTENT MARKETING

Developing interactive content, such as online calculators, interactive infographics or dynamic ebooks, can be an effective way to attract leads. This type of content is not only more engaging, but can also be customized to collect specific information from users, helping to qualify leads.

PARTNERSHIPS WITH OTHER COMPANIES

Identify non-competing companies that offer complementary products or services to yours and explore cross-promotion opportunities. This could include content exchanges, shared product bundles or joint events, expanding the reach of both companies and accessing new groups of potential customers.

REFERRAL MARKETING

Encouraging your existing customers to refer new customers can be one of the most effective and low-cost ways to generate leads. Offer incentives to both the referrer and the referred to motivate participation and ensure that both see value in the transaction.

Generating leads requires a combination of strategy, creativity and a willingness to try new approaches. By implementing these creative ideas, you can not only increase your lead base but also strengthen your brand presence and build more meaningful relationships with your customers.

The next chapter, **SELLING WITHOUT SELLING** , will focus on how to approach prospecting and sales in a way that minimizes pressure and maximizes value for your prospects, creating a more authentic and satisfying experience for both parties. Get ready to explore techniques that allow you to sell more effectively while maintaining integrity and authenticity in every interaction.

SELLING WITHOUT SELLING

The art of selling without appearing to be selling, also known as consultative selling or value-based selling, is a crucial skill in building lasting relationships and achieving sustainable sales success. This chapter explores how you can approach prospecting and sales in a way that naturally leads to conversion, without directly putting pressure on the customer, creating an authentic and satisfying experience for both parties.

FOCUSING ON THE SOLUTION, NOT THE PRODUCT

An effective approach is to focus on understanding the customer's problems or needs and then presenting your offering as the solution. This means actively listening during conversations, asking pertinent questions to deepen your understanding, and then personalizing your communication to show how your product or service can meet your customer's specific needs.

BUILDING RELATIONSHIPS, NOT MAKING TRANSACTIONS

Prioritize the long-term relationship rather than focusing on the immediate transaction. Show genuine interest in the customer's success and be willing to offer help or advice, even if it doesn't immediately result in a sale. This approach builds trust and credibility, increasing the chances that the customer will come to you when they are ready to buy.

EDUCATION AS A SALES TOOL

Providing educational content that helps customers better understand their own problem and possible solutions can be a powerful way to sell without selling. Webinars, e-books, case studies, and blogs are effective tools for educating your audience, establishing your brand as a trusted source of information and a valuable partner.

USING FEEDBACK AND TESTIMONIALS

Sharing success stories and testimonials from satisfied customers can be a subtle way to sell your product or service, allowing the experiences of others to speak for the quality and effectiveness of your offering. This not only demonstrates the value of what you are offering, but also reduces the customer's perception of risk.

OFFERING FREE TRIALS OR DEMONSTRATIONS

Allowing potential customers to try your product or service without commitment can be an effective way to sell without pressure. Whether you offer a trial, free samples, or a demo, you give your customer the chance to see the value of your offering for themselves.

LISTENING AND ADAPTING

Pay attention to customer signals and be ready to adapt your approach. If a potential customer doesn't seem interested or ready to buy, don't force the sale. Instead, ask how you can be helpful in other ways or if there's a better time to resume the conversation.

BEING TRANSPARENT

Transparency about pricing, features, and any limitations of your product or service can reinforce customer trust and demonstrate integrity. Customers value honesty and are more likely to do business with companies that treat them with respect and openness.

Selling without selling is about creating value, establishing trust and cultivating relationships. By focusing on understanding and meeting your customers' needs, you not only improve the shopping experience for them, but you also lay the foundation for the long-term success of your business.

Moving forward, the next chapter, **NEGOTIATION AND CLOSING SALES**, will dive into the techniques and strategies for effectively negotiating and closing sales, ensuring you can convert prospects into paying customers efficiently and ethically. Get ready to improve your negotiation and closing skills, crucial for any sales professional.

NEGOTIATION AND CLOSING SALES

The final phase of the sales process, negotiation and closing, is where all your skills and previous efforts are put to the test. This chapter focuses on effective strategies for negotiating favorable terms and closing sales efficiently and ethically, ensuring customer satisfaction and forming a solid foundation for lasting relationships.

ESTABLISHING TRUST AND CREDIBILITY

Success in negotiation begins long before discussing specific terms. Throughout the entire sales process, it is crucial to build trust and establish your credibility. This is achieved through in-depth understanding of customer needs, transparent communication and consistent demonstration of the value your offering brings.

UNDERSTANDING CUSTOMER NEEDS

Effective negotiation requires a clear understanding of the client's priorities and limitations. Before entering into the negotiation, make sure you know their goals, what they value most in your offer, and what their pressure points are. This allows you to adapt your proposal in a way that aligns the benefits of your product or service with the customer's specific needs.

NEGOCIATION TECHNIQUES

- **Listen more, talk less:** The ability to listen actively during a negotiation is more valuable than the ability to speak persuasively. By listening, you can identify the client's true interests and adapt your proposal to meet those interests.

- **Create win-win options:** Look for ways to expand the 'pie' rather than just dividing what's on the table. This may involve offering creative solutions that meet the customer's needs while protecting their interests.

- **Be prepared to make concessions:** Know in advance which aspects of your offer are negotiable and how far you can go.

Offering strategic concessions can help facilitate a deal, as long as they don't compromise the core value of what you're offering.

CLOSING THE SALE

Closing the sale is as much about timing as it is about technique. Identify signs that the customer is ready to buy, such as specific questions about pricing or implementation, and be prepared to offer a clear call to action.

- **Summarize the benefits:** Reiterate the value your solution offers by summarizing the key benefits and how they meet the customer's identified needs.

- **Resolve any remaining objections:** Before finalizing the sale, be sure to address and resolve any remaining objections the customer may have.

- **Propose the next step:** Be specific about what happens next, guiding the customer through the final steps of the purchasing process.

AFTER SALES

The sales process does not end with the signing of the contract. Post-sales follow-up is crucial to ensure customer satisfaction, resolve any issues that arise and lay the foundation for future sales or upselling . Keep lines of communication open and regularly check in on how the customer is doing with your solution.

Negotiation and closing sales require a combination of preparation, understanding customer needs, communication skills and timing. By approaching this final phase of the sales process with empathy, ethics and a focus on creating value, you can close more sales and build lasting relationships with your customers.

Moving forward, the next chapter, **SELF-CARE AND STRESS**

MANAGEMENT IN SALES, will highlight the importance of maintaining personal well-being in the high-pressure sales environment, offering strategies for managing stress and maintaining productivity. Get ready to discover how to balance sales success with health and personal satisfaction.

SELF-CARE AND STRESS MANAGEMENT IN SALES

A career in sales, although rewarding, can be a source of significant stress due to constant goal pressures, frequent rejection and the need to always perform at your best. This chapter addresses the importance of self-care and stress management, offering practical strategies for sales professionals to maintain their physical and mental well-being, ensuring not only sales success, but also personal health and satisfaction.

RECOGNIZING STRESS

The first step to managing stress is recognizing it. This can manifest itself in several ways, including tiredness, irritability, anxiety, difficulty concentrating, among others. Accepting that stress is a part of life and a career in sales allows you to take a proactive approach to managing it.

SELF-CARE STRATEGIES

- **Regular exercise:** Physical activity is an effective way to reduce stress. Find a form of exercise that you enjoy, whether it's running, yoga or cycling, and incorporate it regularly into your routine.

- **Healthy eating:** A balanced diet can positively influence your energy and mood. Prioritize nutrient-rich foods and stay hydrated.

- **Quality sleep:** Ensuring a good night's sleep is crucial for managing stress. Establish a relaxing bedtime routine and try to maintain a consistent bedtime and wake-up time.

STRESS MANAGEMENT TECHNIQUES

- **Meditation and mindfulness:** Meditation and mindfulness practices can help calm the mind and reduce stress. Even a few minutes a day can make a significant difference.

- **Time for hobbies and interests:** Making time for activities you love outside of work can help you decompress and maintain a work-life balance.

- **Support network:** Having a support network, whether of colleagues, friends or family, is essential. Sharing experiences and challenges can provide relief and new perspectives.

ESTABLISHING LIMITS

Learning to establish healthy boundaries between work and personal life is essential for managing stress. This may include setting specific times to check work emails, saying no to unrealistic demands, and ensuring enough time for rest and leisure.

REFLECTION AND ADJUSTMENT

Allow yourself regular moments to reflect on your well-being and progress with self-care strategies. Be kind to yourself and recognize that managing stress is an ongoing process. Be open to adjusting your strategies as needed to find what works best for you.

Taking care of yourself is essential to maintaining productivity and satisfaction in a career in sales. By adopting self-care and stress management strategies, you can face the challenges inherent to the profession more effectively, ensuring not only success in sales, but also a more balanced and rewarding life.

Moving on, the next and final chapter, **30-DAY ACTION PLAN FOR ACTIVE PROSPECTION**, will provide a step-by-step guide to putting into practice the strategies and insights discussed throughout the book, helping you start building your customer base now. Get ready to chart a clear path toward prospecting success.

30-DAY ACTION PLAN FOR ACTIVE PROSPECTION

This final chapter provides a concrete, structured action plan for the next 30 days, designed to help you implement the active prospecting strategies discussed throughout this book. By following this step-by-step guide, you can start building and expanding your customer base in an effective and systematic way.

DAY 1-5: PREPARATION AND PLANNING

- **Day 1:** Review and define your prospecting objectives. What are your sales goals for the next 30 days? Be specific and measurable.

- **Day 2:** Conduct market research and identify your target audience. Who are your ideal customers? What are your needs and pain points?

- **Day 3:** Develop your value proposition. Why should potential customers choose you? How can you uniquely solve their problems?

- **Day 4:** Prepare your prospecting material. This can include cold calling scripts, email templates, and educational or promotional content.

- **Day 5:** Organize your tools and resources. Make sure your CRM is up to date, set up any necessary automation software, and plan your daily prospecting routine.

DAY 6-10: INITIAL IMPLEMENTATION

- **Day 6-7:** Initiate cold calling activities based on your research and preparation. Focus on actively listening and adapting your approach as needed.

- **Day 8:** Send your first batches of prospecting emails. Use the prepared templates, but personalize each message for the recipient.

- **Day 9:** Engage with potential customers on social media. Comment on relevant posts, join groups in your industry and share valuable content.

- **Day 10:** Evaluate and adjust your prospecting strategies. What worked well? what can be improved?

DAY 11-20: EXPANSION AND OPTIMIZATION

- **Day 11-15:** Continue with prospecting activities, gradually increasing the volume as you become more comfortable and efficient in your approaches.

- **Day 16:** Implement a content strategy focused on generating leads. This could include posting an informative blog, launching a webinar, or publishing a case study.

- **Day 17-18:** Explore new prospecting channels. This may involve partnerships with influencers, participation in virtual events, or paid advertising campaigns.

- **Day 19-20:** Carry out strategic follow-ups. Use insights from past interactions to personalize your messages and offers.

DAY 21-30: CONTINUOUS ASSESSMENT AND ADJUSTMENT

- **Day 21-25:** Maintain a steady pace of prospecting activities, incorporating feedback and learnings from your previous efforts.

- **Day 26:** Collect and analyze data. Review the prospecting KPIs initially established and evaluate their performance.

- **Day 27-28:** Make adjustments based on your analysis. Refine your strategies, messages and approaches as needed.

- **Day 29:** Plan your next steps. Based on your progress, set goals for the next month.

- **Day 30:** Set aside time for reflection and self-care. Recognize your efforts and successes, and make sure you take care of your mental and physical health.

This 30-day action plan is a starting point for you to implement and improve your active prospecting strategies. Remember that prospecting is an ongoing process that requires adaptation, learning, and persistence. By following this guide, you will be well equipped to build a solid customer base and drive your business growth.

As we turn the final page of this journey together, I sincerely hope that the learnings shared here have touched your heart and sparked new perspectives. If this book has brought you any value, I kindly ask that you take a few moments to leave a review on Amazon. Your words not only help me grow and hone my craft, but they also guide other readers in their quests for knowledge and inspiration. Your opinion is a valuable gift, both for me and for the community of readers looking for stories that transform. I sincerely thank you for sharing this journey with me and I hope we can meet again in the pages of a new adventure.

REGINALDO OSNILDO

Hello, I'm Reginaldo Osnildo, author and innovator in the fields of sales, technology, and communication strategies. My background spans from the academic setting, as a professor and researcher at the University of Southern Santa Catarina, to hands-on strategy development at the Catarinense Radio Group. With a PhD in sales narratives and digital convergence, and a Master's in storytelling and social imaginary, I offer my readers a unique blend of theory and practice. My aim is to deliver knowledge in a simple, practical, and didactic language, encouraging direct application in one's personal and professional life.

Yours sincerely

Reginaldo Osnildo

+55 48 991913865

reginaldoosnildo@gmail.com

www.ingramcontent.com/pod-product-compliance
Lightning Source LLC
Chambersburg PA
CBHW050328230526
45471CB00005B/2401